To Leah
With much love,
Margo & Jacqi

Durrell McKenna, Nancy
Canadian family.—(Beans).
1. Canada—Social life and customs—1941–
Juvenile literature
I. Title
871.064'7 F1021·2

ISBN 0–7136–2978–9

A & C Black (Publishers) Limited
35 Bedford Row, London WC1R 4JH



Acknowledgements
Designed by Robert Wheeler
The map is by Tony Garrett



Filmset by August Filmsetting, Haydock, St Helens
Printed in Hong Kong by Dai Nippon Printing Co. Ltd

# Canadian Family

Nancy Durrell McKenna

A & C Black · London

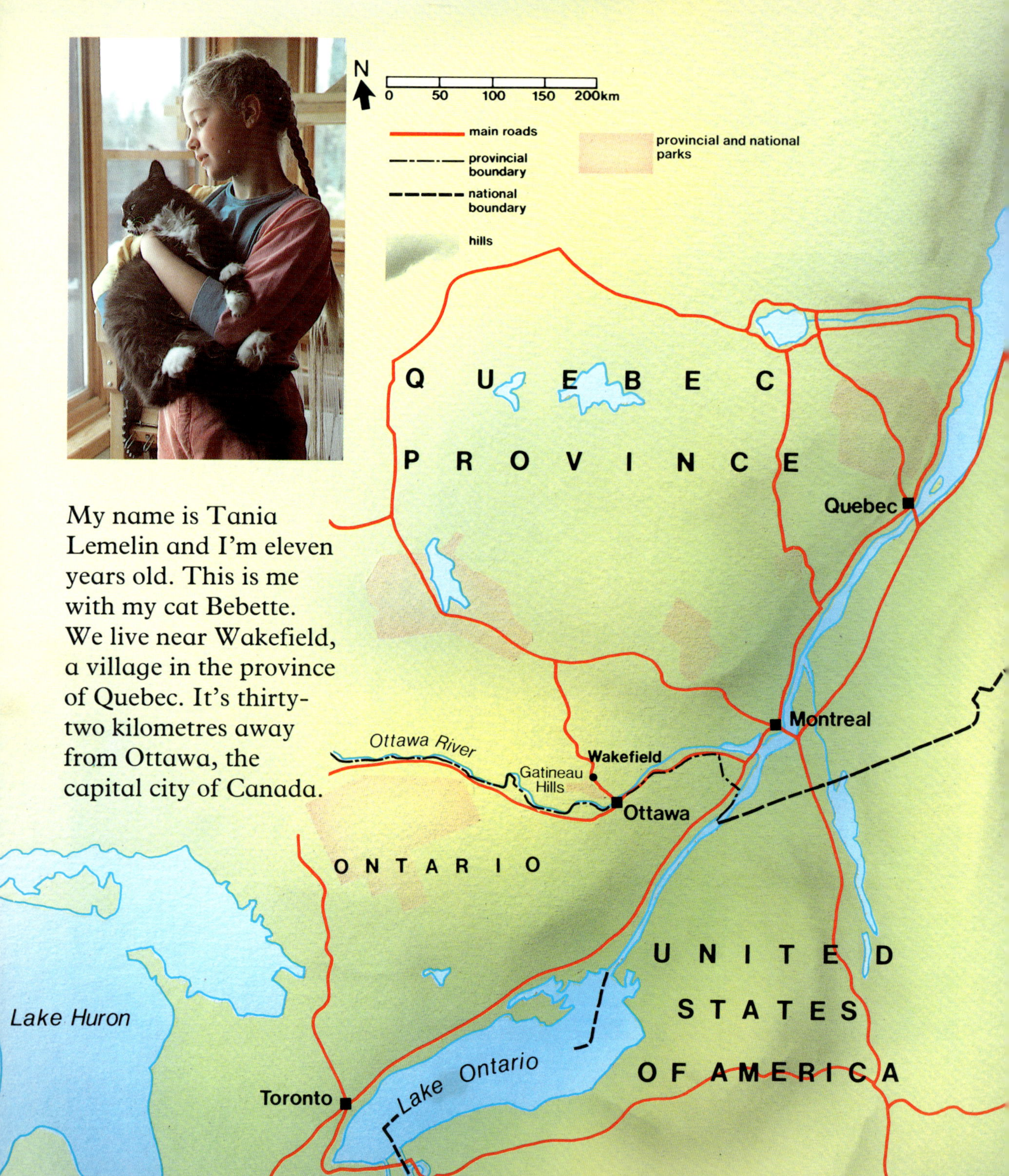


My name is Tania Lemelin and I'm eleven years old. This is me with my cat Bebette. We live near Wakefield, a village in the province of Quebec. It's thirty-two kilometres away from Ottawa, the capital city of Canada.

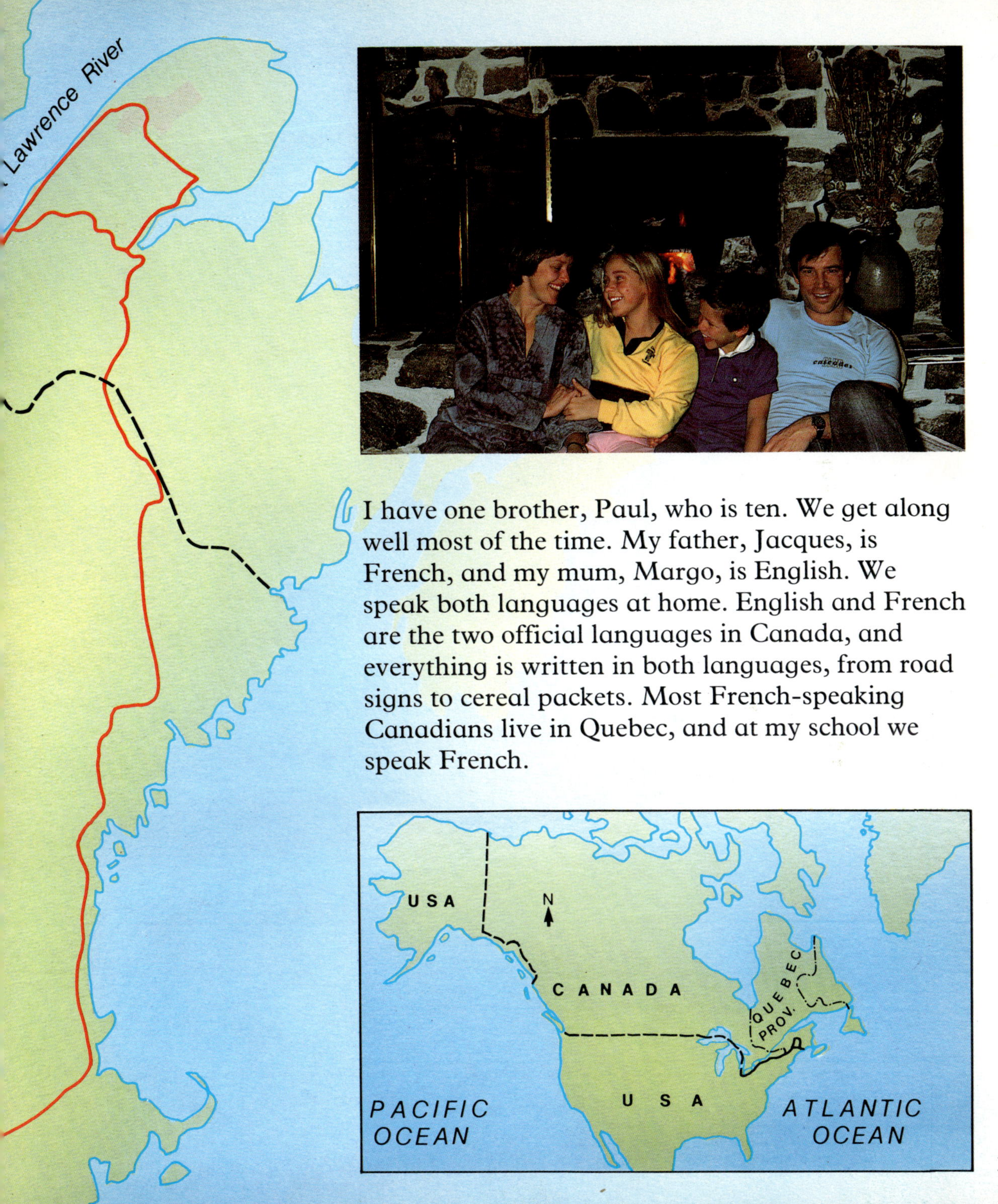


I have one brother, Paul, who is ten. We get along well most of the time. My father, Jacques, is French, and my mum, Margo, is English. We speak both languages at home. English and French are the two official languages in Canada, and everything is written in both languages, from road signs to cereal packets. Most French-speaking Canadians live in Quebec, and at my school we speak French.

I remember watching our house being built. It's on a hill in the countryside and Mum and Papa got the wood from a one hundred year old barn. Papa is always adding to the house – he built the porch last spring. There are three other houses on our road but we can't see them because of the trees – we own five acres of land covered by woods.

In winter it gets really cold outside – the temperature is usually −20° centigrade. The snow gets very deep and if Papa didn't use the snow-blower on the front path, the snow would reach the top of the front door.

Just after the snow has fallen, it's too fluffy to make a snowman. When it is wet and heavy, we all go out and start building a giant one. We gave this one an old scarf of Paul's and one of Papa's old hats. We finished him off by giving him a potato for a nose.

Sometimes the weather gets as cold as −30°. When it's that cold we can't play outside, so we play in the huge basement of our house. There's a family rule that we don't watch television during the week, but I don't have much time anyway, because I have to do my homework and piano practice. I'm also teaching myself to type on our computer, instead of just using it to play games and draw pictures.

I have my own bedroom, and when I want to be alone to read or just to think, I go up to my room. My favourite books are adventure stories like 'Swallows and Amazons', and 'The Lion, the Witch and the Wardrobe'.

At weekends we often rent a video, make a fire and heat up a big bowl of popcorn. It's great to feel cosy and warm, watching a movie while the snow falls outside. I like comedies and mystery movies best.

My school is called Ecole Lapeche. It's six kilometres from home so Paul and I go there by bus. Papa drives us to the bus stop on his way to work.

School starts at half past eight. I'm in the fifth grade, and the year after next I'll be going to Junior High.

My favourite subjects are maths, art and PE. We have all our lessons in French, except English lessons of course. English classes are easy for me because I speak English at home and most of my friends don't.

In French classes we have a different theme each week. This time it's 'le poisson' or fish. Our teacher, Suzanne sets us questions to do. She's always there to help us if we need it. We work in groups and help each other to find the answers. I usually try to work with my best friend Nancy. I work hard because I want to go to college when I'm older.

After school Paul and I have to walk home from the bus stop. It's a fifteen minute walk but often we take longer because we play on the way. In winter we have snowball fights and make snow angels.

Every day during termtime I do extra activities after school. On Mondays I go to the Ottawa School of Dance for ballet and jazz dance lessons. I like dance and movement because it helps me to express the way I feel. On my birthday Mum took me to see some professional dancers at the National Arts Centre in Ottawa. I tried to imagine what it would be like to dance as well as they do – they make it look so easy, but I know how difficult it really is.

On Wednesdays, Paul and I have piano lessons. I've just passed my grade three exam - it was nerve-wracking. Before my exam, I tried to practise for forty-five minutes every day, but sometimes Mum or Papa had to remind me to do it.

On Thursdays we go to the Takahashi Dojo for judo lessons. The Dojo is a practice hall where we work on mats to protect ourselves when we get thrown on the ground. Judo makes me feel that I can take care of myself and it keeps me fit.

Dance and judo lessons are in Ottawa which is forty-five minutes drive away. There aren't any buses from home so Mum or Papa have to drive us each time, and pick us up afterwards.

My papa is a family doctor in Wakefield. He works at the Gatineau Memorial hospital, but he also sees sick people at his office or in their homes. Papa says he likes his work because he treats so many different problems, and he sees everyone from old people to new-born babies so he gets to know the families he takes care of.

My mum used to be a teacher, but she gave up when Paul and I were little. When we started school, she learned how to weave. She made beautiful rugs and tapestries on her loom at home.

Now Mum has gone back to university. She spends a lot of time studying for her exams so Papa, Paul and I have to help around the house much more than we used to.

When Mum first went back to being a student, I was worried that we wouldn't have much time together. But I needn't have worried – Mum always makes time for us. Someday I would like to get married and have children as well as having a career of my own, like Mum.

At weekends we often have a late morning meal together - it's too late for breakfast and too early for lunch, so we call it brunch. Papa's speciality is French toast. He makes it by soaking thick slices of bread in a mixture of eggs, milk and cinnamon. Then he fries the bread. We eat it with masses of maple syrup poured over it, and with crispy bacon – yummy.

On some Saturdays I go to the market in Ottawa with Mum. I help her shop for fruit, vegetables, fish and meat, and we get everything else in our local supermarket. I'm learning to compare prices because Mum says soon I can do the shopping on my own.

I enjoy cooking good things to eat, especially cookies and home-fried potatoes. Mum taught me how to make mayonnaise, and now I am responsible for keeping the mayonnaise jar full.

As a weekend treat we go to our local 'Patates Frites' stand. It used to be an old school bus until the owners fixed it up. Now they sell the best chips around.

Usually on winter weekends, Paul and I go skiing. We make a packed lunch for the day, then Mum or Papa drives us to the ski hill. Our nearest one is called Vorlage. Sometimes the whole family skis together, or we meet friends there.

There's a ski-lift to the top of the hill. You sit on a bar and the lift tows you up.

I love the feeling when I'm skiing. I speed down the hill with the wind blowing on my face. It's thrilling to jump from a ski bump, but you have to remember to bend your knees when you land so that you don't break your leg. When we go skiing with Papa we practise a lot of jumping.

Night skiing is really special. We go once a week to Vorlage. All you can see is the slope and the lights down each side. It feels completely different from skiing during the daytime – it's so silent, and very dramatic.

Once a year we go to visit Papa's family in Quebec City. Their house is near a huge mountain which is great for skiing, so we usually go and see them in winter. There are cable cars up the mountain, and most of the slopes take about twenty minutes to ski down. It's far more fun than Vorlage where we get to the bottom in five minutes.

In the summer, my family likes to spend weekends away from home exploring the countryside in Quebec and Ontario. We load up the car with our camping gear and the canoe, and set off for unknown places.

Camping weekends are really special to me – they are times when our family can be together, away from the routines at home.

Paul and I have our own tent which we put up by ourselves. After setting up camp we go for a swim, or we take the canoe out and go fishing. We paddle the canoe North American Indian style, and once we've got a rhythm going, we can be quite fast.

We cook over an open fire, so Paul and I have to search for dry wood which Papa chops with an axe. Meanwhile Mum gets the food ready. If one of us has been lucky and caught a pike or bass in the lake, we eat that. There's nothing better than fresh fish that's been barbequed over a fire.

In the evenings, when the sun has gone down, we sit round the fire and toast marshmallows on long sticks. We sing songs and Papa tells us ghost stories. Later, when Paul and I are curled up in our sleeping bags, we jump at any little noise.

All year long I look forward to the start of the summer holidays in July, when I go to Camp Tawingo in northern Ontario for three weeks. At summer camp I sleep in a cabin with seven other girls my age, and our counsellor who's older.

Paul goes to Tawingo as well, but I don't see him very often. He's in the boys' section and there are more than six hundred campers at Tawingo. I love seeing my old friends from all over Canada, as well as making lots of new ones.

There are lots of activities to do – last year I learned to windsurf. When the wind catches your sail it feels like flying, only on water. I also had a part in a musical of 'Alice in Wonderland', where I was a singing and dancing flower.

I don't have any friends within walking distance of home, so I'm glad that there's a day camp in Wakefield for the rest of the summer. We start each day in the camp garden, even if it's raining, learning to grow vegetables. Best of all I like eating the fresh vegetables, specially peas straight from the pod.

In our free time, Becky, Siobhan and I play around on the swinging tyres. Becky and Siobhan are good friends of mine. They came round to the pyjama party I had for my birthday. We watched a scary video and stayed up late, talking and telling jokes.

My birthday is on August 5th so the week before Mum took me to Ottawa as a treat to choose a present.

I couldn't decide whether to have a baggy green sweater or a new watch. In the end, as you can see, I chose the sweater. Perhaps I'll save up for the watch – I get an allowance of two dollars a week.

The biggest choice of shops is at the Rideau Centre, which is huge and has more than two hundred shops inside. There are glass-covered walkways between different parts of the centre so that you can go shopping even if it's snowing or raining hard outside.

Shopping makes me hungry, so we stopped for doughnuts and a coke before going to look at the Parliament Buildings where the Government of Canada meets.

I talked to Mum about what I want to do when I grow up. I'd like to be a lawyer or an actress – actually to be a lawyer, you have to be a good actress so that you can present your case well.

This year Mum and Papa decided that Paul and I were old enough to go camping with them in the wilderness. We went to the real wilderness where there aren't any roads or people, and we had to be flown in by seaplane. Our guide, Bill Bale, is seventy-five. He helped us to get ready for the trip. We were going to be alone for five days so it was important that we didn't forget anything we'd need, like matches.

It was the first time I'd ever been in a small plane, and it was terrific. I felt every movement in my stomach. We flew so low that I could see the lakes and forests very clearly.

Before we could explore, we had to set up camp. Paul and I fetched water from the lake. It is so clean that we didn't have to boil it before drinking.

That afternoon, I caught the first fish of the trip – a huge pike. It turned out to be the biggest fish anyone caught on the whole trip. We had it for supper with lots of potatoes. I still had to do the washing up afterwards. That was one of my jobs.

At the end of the week, I saw a moose while we were out canoeing. It was eating the roots of water lilies. I couldn't wait to tell Siobhan. The five days in the wilderness were great, and it was hard to leave our campsite – in just a week it had become our home.